T0129199

HOW TO KILL THE SCRUM MONSTER

QUICK START TO AGILE SCRUM METHODOLOGY AND THE SCRUM MASTER ROLE

Ilya Bibik

Apress®

How to Kill the Scrum Monster: Quick Start to Agile Scrum Methodology and the Scrum Master Role

Ilya Bibik
Montreal, Québec, Canada

ISBN-13 (pbk): 978-1-4842-3690-1   ISBN-13 (electronic): 978-1-4842-3691-8
https://doi.org/10.1007/978-1-4842-3691-8

Library of Congress Control Number: 2018947389

Managing Director, Apress Media LLC: Welmoed Spahr
Acquisitions Editor: Shiva Ramachandran
Development Editor: Laura Berendson
Coordinating Editor: Rita Fernando

Cover designed by eStudioCalamar

Distributed to the book trade worldwide by Springer Science+Business Media New York, 233 Spring Street, 6th Floor, New York, NY 10013. Phone 1-800-SPRINGER, fax (201) 348-4505, e-mail orders-ny@springer-sbm.com, or visit www.springeronline.com. Apress Media, LLC is a California LLC and the sole member (owner) is Springer Science + Business Media Finance Inc (SSBM Finance Inc). SSBM Finance Inc is a **Delaware** corporation.

For information on translations, please e-mail rights@apress.com, or visit www.apress.com/rights-permissions.

Apress titles may be purchased in bulk for academic, corporate, or promotional use. eBook versions and licenses are also available for most titles. For more information, reference our Print and eBook Bulk Sales web page at www.apress.com/bulk-sales.

Any source code or other supplementary material referenced by the author in this book is available to readers on GitHub via the book's product page, located at www.apress.com/9781484236901. For more detailed information, please visit www.apress.com/source-code.

Printed on acid-free paper

Contents

About the Author. v

Acknowledgments vii

Introduction ix

Chapter 1: From Waterfall to Agile. 1

Chapter 2: Overview of Agile Methodologies. 7

Chapter 3: Agile Scrum Deep Dive. 15

Chapter 4: Scrum Master: What It's All About 31

Chapter 5: Team Dynamics 39

Chapter 6: Key Takeaways 51

Appendix A: Case Studies. 53

Index 75

About the Author

Ilya Bibik is an experienced Scrum Master with more than 16 years of experience in the software development industry, including seven years in the Scrum Master role. He has a master's degree in e-commerce and a bachelor's degree in software engineering, and a teaching diploma. His professional background includes software development, software project management, software quality management, software security, software sales, school teaching, and military experience with electro-optical technologies.

During his career in the software industry, Ilya has used software development methodologies such as Scrum, Kanban, and Waterfall. He has worked on software projects in the areas of retail, wholesale, fashion, e-commerce, e-learning, manufacturing, ISO-9000, and rental property management. For additional content from the author about Scrum methodology and to contact Ilya please refer to http://scrumyes.com/.

Acknowledgments

This book is dedicated to my parents, Yaara and Victor; and to my sister, Anna, to whom I owe everything; and to my kids, Basil, Michael, and Evan, whom I am blessed to have around and watch them grow!

I want to say thank you to all the people who helped me. First, thanks to my great wife, Marianna Levant, for her support of the idea and original editing and feedback when I wrote my first draft during my commute on the train.

Thanks go to my manager, Camille El Gammal, and my colleague, Scrum Master Parinaz Barakhshan, who reviewed the first version and gave me their supportive feedback and comments on the book.

And I am thankful to have worked with the crew from Apress: acquisition editor Shiva Ramachandran, who gave me the opportunity to publish with Apress; coordiating editor Rita Fernando Kim, who made things fast and simple; and development editor, Laura Berendson.

I also want to thank all the people I worked with at SAP Labs Canada at the Montreal location who tolerated me for almost 11 years and allowed me to gain experience on different topics.

Introduction

After working seven years as a Scrum Master, I decided to create an easy-to-consume, concise, and programmatic book covering what is necessary. This book is a practical and pragmatic guide to the implementation of Scrum methodology in the team—not only the theory, but the real-life problems of working with real people rather than with the imaginary ideal teams that do not exist. The book focuses on the Scrum Master role because it is key to a successful implementation of the Scrum methodology.

The target audience of this book is anyone who is new to the topic and interested in understanding what the Scrum methodology is all about. The book also will be of use to anyone who is looking for ways to kill the existing Scrum monster if you are struggling to adopt Scrum in your organization. Also, this book will help to get a better understanding of Scrum Master role importance and role challenges.

There are other agile methodologies on the market and I mention some of them in this book—Kanban, Scrumban, eXtreme programming—in the context of Scrum.

I aim to answer the following questions:

- What is Agile? (from Waterfall to the Agile Manifesto and how Agile can become a problem instead of a solution)

- What is the Scrum Methodology and how does it relate to eXtreme and Kanban?

- What are the Scrum Master challenges?

- What are the team development stages?

- What methods exist to handle conflicts in the team?

From Waterfall to Agile

Before Agile came into the picture, the most common methodology of software development was Waterfall. Waterfall is a model in which the project is planned and executed within a time period that is required to achieve the final goal.

That means, when we are talking about big projects that typically take a few years to complete, **we might only be able to see result in a few years**. Usually, waterfall translates into dividing the project into phases based on the work type: capture the requirements, design the architecture, develop the software, and finally test and deploy (Figure 1-1).

© Ilya Bibik 2018
I. Bibik, How to Kill the Scrum Monster, https://doi.org/10.1007/978-1-4842-3691-8_1

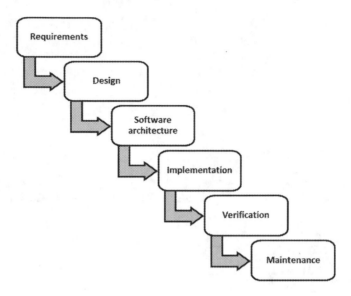

Figure 1-1. Waterfall model

The issue with this methodology is that if a project has a big scope, it might take many months if not years until we get final results. A lot of things can change and go the wrong way. Sometimes during the final stage of acceptance and testing, we might discover that the original design stage was wrong. The success rate of a big project executed in this way is alarmingly low (Figure 1-2).

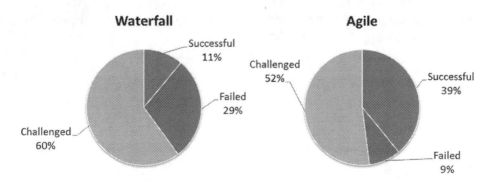

Figure 1-2. Waterfall vs. Agile (Source: The Standish Group 2015 Chaos Report)

From this archaic environment, 17 experienced and tired software veterans created the Agile Manifesto and totally changed the game. Before the Agile Manifesto had been adopted, the software development process was not too flexible and was very long; however, after introduction of the Agile concept, the development process became faster and more flexible and able to adapt to constantly changing reality.

The Agile Manifesto that was published in 2001 is just a set of 12 principles and values, rather than actual methodologies or a framework.

I've reproduced it here in its entirety because so many people who promote it, consult on the subject, or claim they are following the principles have never actually read it, or if they have read it, may not understand it. Bottom line: before you continue reading this book or getting familiar with Agile or any Agile methodology, read the manifesto completely and be inspired. If you think you are already following Agile methodology but this manifesto doesn't align with your current methods, it **could only mean one thing—you are not really following Agile principles.**

MANIFESTO FOR AGILE SOFTWARE DEVELOPMENT[1]

We are uncovering better ways of developing software by doing it and helping others do it. Through this work we have come to value:

Individuals and interactions over processes and tools

Working software over comprehensive documentation

Customer collaboration over contract negotiation

Responding to change over following a plan

That is, while there is value in the items on the right, we value the items on the left more.

Kent Beck	James Grenning	Robert C. Martin
Mike Beedle	Jim Highsmith	Steve Mellor
Arie van Bennekum	Andrew Hunt	Ken Schwaber
Alistair Cockburn	Ron Jeffries	Jeff Sutherland
Ward Cunningham	Jon Kern	Dave Thomas
Martin Fowler	Brian Marick	

© 2001, the above authors

This declaration may be freely copied in any form, but only in its entirety through this notice.

---

[1]http://agilemanifesto.org/

PRINCIPLES BEHIND THE AGILE MANIFESTO[2]

We follow these principles:

Our highest priority is to satisfy the customer through early and continuous delivery of valuable software.

Welcome changing requirements, even late in development. Agile processes harness change for the customer's competitive advantage.

Deliver working software frequently, from a couple of weeks to a couple of months, with a preference to the shorter timescale.

Business people and developers must work together daily throughout the project.

Build projects around motivated individuals. Give them the environment and support they need, and trust them to get the job done.

The most efficient and effective method of conveying information to and within a development team is face-to-face conversation.

Working software is the primary measure of progress.

Agile processes promote sustainable development. The sponsors, developers, and users should be able to maintain a constant pace indefinitely.

Continuous attention to technical excellence and good design enhances agility.

Simplicity—the art of maximizing the amount of work not done—is essential.

The best architectures, requirements, and designs emerge from self-organizing teams.

At regular intervals, the team reflects on how to become more effective, then tunes and adjusts its behavior accordingly.

© 2001, the above authors

This declaration may be freely copied in any form, but only in its entirety through this notice.

So there you have it. Did you get the idea that the Agile Manifesto is the cornerstone of Agile? The Agile Manifesto is not a framework, nor is it a methodology—it is just common sense that was put into words and sentences by a group of experts from the industry who were tired of Waterfall processes that didn't always work.

But....

As it often happens with a good simple concept, the software industry created a **monster**.

---

[2]http://agilemanifesto.org/principles.html

Agile was supposed to be a set of principles and values that help us to deliver, embrace change, and be responsive. Instead we got a lot of methodologies, certifications, and terms, and behind all this noise often the main ideas from the manifesto gets lost. So instead of improving productivity and quality, implementing Agile methodology can result in unnecessary waste and additional frustration to the team. Let's look at the most commonly used Agile Methodologies - Scrum.

Here are some examples of Scrum misuse:

- Endless discussions on some details on how to assign story points, or argument that some team rituals are not Agile according to some mysterious books and experts.

- So-called Scrum experts who insist on using the methods they picked up after reading one or two books on the subject and will radicalize you in case you run the meetings without fancy methods they remember.

- Religious creation of a burndown chart that eventually becomes the goal of the Sprint rather than delivering actual software.

- Endless exhausting meetings that have no clear purpose.

All this doesn't help with adoption of Agile methodology in the teams.

Often, teams that want to adopt Agile methodology become overwhelmed and things get worse instead of better.

It doesn't mean that people who promote some particular Agile methodology in certain way have bad intentions. It, however, does mean that repeating some successful rituals from one team to another will not necessarily bring the desired result.

As an illustration: During WW2 some Melanesian islands became bases for Japanese and, later, Allied forces. Locals were exposed to airplanes and western civilization for the first time. The military shared their food supplies and other items with the locals, and the islanders became accustomed to western goods. After the war, the troops abandoned the bases and the islands were forgotten.

Years later, research expeditions visited the islands and they saw that the locals were imitating military rituals and had built runways and airplane idols out of wood. The locals expected that if they performed the routine that had been there during presence of military on the islands, the airplanes would return and bring them cargo. This phenomenon has been named a *Cargo Cult*.

The religious following of some Agile methods that worked for some teams at certain point is also a form of Cargo Cult.

It is expected that if all the rituals and terminologies of the holy Agile methodologies are respected religiously (without necessarily understanding the reasoning behind them), the miracle of productivity and success will happen.

Unfortunately, in most situations, it is not the case and the opposite might be a likely outcome.

Prior to experimentation or discussing any fancy buzz methods of Agile methodologies, decision-makers and the team should get familiar with most basic Agile principles from the Manifesto. And only after that, the team can start exploring popular Agile techniques and decide if they have any real value in order to solve problems they encounter.

Overview of Agile Methodologies

Before jumping into the Agile Scrum methodology and Scrum Master role description, let's have an overview of the most common Agile methodologies to get some context so we do not operate in a vacuum.

There are three most common methodologies/methods to implement Agile principles: eXtreme programming, Scrum, and Kanban.

We can classify those in a scale from more prescriptive to more adaptive. So eXtreme programming (XP) is a very strict process that enforces a lot of rules and regulations on how things should be done, and Kanban is something with the minimum amount of sets and regulations. Scrum is in the middle and can shift to be less or more prescriptive based on the need (Figure 2-1).

© Ilya Bibik 2018
I. Bibik, How to Kill the Scrum Monster, https://doi.org/10.1007/978-1-4842-3691-8_2

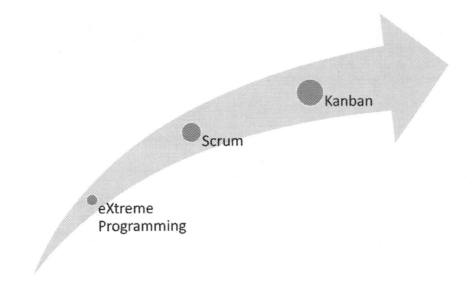

Figure 2-1. Moving from prescriptive to more adaptive

Let's have a more detailed look at each methodology mentioned.

eXtreme Programming

XP is the most prescriptive (specific) of the Agile methodologies, for which the main focus is **prescription of engineering** processes.

XP usually works in short development cycles of one week, so that changes requested by the customer can be frequently incorporated. The whole team works as one without having defined roles, and the customer becomes part of the team.

XP prescribes many core practices, which include test-driven development, customer testing, continuous integration, short iterations, small releases, pair programming, planning game, simple design, refactoring, collective code ownership, coding standards, metaphor, sustainable pace, customer working closely on site with the team, and customer acceptance test on each release.

Eventually, it all should translate to high quality of code produced. Despite the claims that XP is more productive in XP-oriented resources, development can be slower than other methodologies. I believe it can be more productive only in some specific cases.

The main difference from Scrum: I find XP more driven by code development methodologies rather than team dynamics and processes within the team. XP has a less flexible framework than Scrum. Scrum can adopt practices from XP and basically do the same thing as XP but when required, Scrum is flexible enough to switch to less prescriptive methodology like Kanban. Scrum is more focused on productivity, while XP is focused on engineering.

If you do want your team to use XP methodology eventually, Scrum can be an intermediate step; the team can start using Scrum and gradually adopt XP best practices.

Risks and Mitigations

Risk of wasting capacity: Some of those prescriptive engineering processes applied to XP might bring very little to no value.

Mitigation: In cases where quality is not a life-critical process, Scrum methodology can be a better suited methodology.

Risk of lack of customer availability: Since customers can't always commit to becoming part of the team, it can become an issue for XP methodology.

Mitigation: Rely more on Scrum methodology, where the Product Owner (PO) can substitute for lack of customer commitment, to a certain extent.

Kanban

Kanban was invented by Toyota in the 1940s to reduce idle time during manufacturing. In the software world, it is basically executing work as it comes and using a board with notes to track the progress and bottlenecks.

Kanban is all about visualization of the process, so the expression "a picture is worth a thousand words" really describes the Kanban process very accurately (Figure 2-2).

New	Analysis in Process	Analysis Done	Development in Process	Development Done	Test	Deploy
						Feature 1 (Bob)
		Feature 2 (Bob)				
				Feature 3 (Alice)		
						Feature 4 (Yevgen)
Feature 5						
Feature 6						
Feature 7						

Figure 2-2. Kanban board example

The work doesn't have to come in iterations in Kanban, and this process is very suitable for **support** activities or in some cases for SaaS cloud based solutions.

The roles in the team are not necessarily defined: everybody does everything.

Kanban mainly concentrates on work process. It can be good practice to have some elements of Scrum methodology, like a daily **Scrum meeting** if required. The main strength of Kanban is a **visualization** of the work process that helps the team to identify **bottlenecks or opportunities to reduce idle time**. For example, instead of continuing with developing, all the team members will start just testing if they see that the amount of testing tasks piles up.

On the surface the Kanban board may look like a regular task board, with one difference—in Kanban the number of items that can be in progress at any given time is strictly limited to **one or two** tasks each team member can process in parallel.

Despite the board being the center of Kanban methodology, it can also be executed without the actual physical board. When all the team members operate remotely, tools such as **Trello** can be used. Or in some other cases, by just assigning **incidents** to team members, the same goal is achieved without the need of having a physical or even virtual board.

Kanban is really easy to implement in the team; the process is very simple. So even though this book is about Scrum methodology, you should always consider Kanban as a possible solution for your needs in certain situations. For example, during the **maintenance** or **testing phase**, it makes more sense to use Kanban than having an overhead with Scrum methodology.

Risks and Mitigations

Risk of missing the big picture: Kanban takes each task separately and as result, often design, development, and test are on the granularity of this one task. The downside is that an individual team member can be successful in developing this one task feature but will fail on the big picture of how all the features will come together.

Mitigation: In case of a new complex development, rely more on Scrum methodology than on Kanban.

Risk of lack of responsibility: Due to lack of roles, there is no individual responsibility for different parts of the development process, which can result in failure of satisfying customer needs and **quality** issues.

Mitigation: In case of a new complex development, rely more on Scrum methodology than on Kanban, or at least have some accountable roles.

Scrum

Scrum is one of the most popular, if not *the* most popular, of Agile methodologies. Similar to XP, it has short releases. Those iterations are called Sprints. It has roles in the team such as Scrum Master(in charge of the process) and Product Owner (in charge of the product); there are also other defined roles in the team. It also includes mandatory meetings: Daily Scrum (stand-up meeting), Planning, Review, Retrospective, and Backlog Grooming.

We will discuss Scrum methodology in detail in later chapters of this book.

The main advantage of Scrum and why I am advocating it over XP and Kanban is that Scrum can incorporate the best of both words of Kanban and XP, based on the situation and needs.

Risks and Mitigations

Risk of meetings overkill: Meeting rituals are not always relevant to everyone, and can be demotivating and unnecessary.

Mitigation: Scrum Masters require meeting moderation skills.

Risk of changes during the Sprint: Scope changes during the Sprint execution can lead to an unsuccessful Sprint and waste, since they can result in duplication of meetings and discussion.

Mitigation: Embrace the change with a positive attitude; better to do it in the middle of the Sprint then after the Sprint. However, Scrum Master meeting moderation skill is a must to reduce the meetings durations as much as possible. As well be clear to highlight the issues and be transparent with stakeholders on **how changes affect capacity**.

Risk of estimation: Inaccurate estimations can lead to wrong assumptions and failed Sprints. As well, estimation during meetings can lead to long meetings and demotivation.

Mitigation: Scrum Master meeting moderation skill—high-level estimate. Keeping some buffer and committing to fewer tasks during the Sprint but having a few extra tasks in case of additional capacity.

Hybrid of Different Methodologies

Different methodologies can be modified and combined together in order to address particular problems that have to be resolved.

Scrumban, for example, as the name suggests is a mix between Scrum and Kanban. From Scrum, it uses the principles of **iterations** to develop new features and from another side, Kanban can be used to provide fixes to existing features. Combined together, this methodology can perfectly fit the needs of the team and delivers **new functionality** and **provides support** to existing functionality.

However, support is not the only case when Scrumban can become handy.

Many projects move to cloud as SaaS solutions. Since running software in the cloud and constantly upgrading it in some cases might be a different process from the standard development where we release software from version to version, a merger of Scrum and Kanban methodologies can be a good fit. **Small features** will be delivered with **Kanban** and **more complex** functionality will be still developed in **Scrum methodology.**

Another case when Scrumban can become handy is when we have a shortage in headcount. Kanban with some elements from Scrum can be a good way to compensate for the lack of resources, since it doesn't require all the roles existing in Scrum.

A mix of Scrum and Kanban is not the only combination possible. eXtreme programming also goes well together with Scrum methodology. We can use many prescribed **XP techniques** as part of Scrum, for example, **continuous integration**, refactoring, and pair programming.

Lean

Lean is not Agile methodology but since we are talking about Agile, it is very probable you've heard the term *Lean* and you may be wondering how it relates to Agile. While the Agile manifesto was originally created for software development, Lean concepts come from **Lean manufacturing** and have been adopted by Mary & Tom Poppendieck to fit software development.[1]

Those principles are:

1. Eliminate Waste
2. Build Quality In
3. Create Knowledge
4. Defer Commitment
5. Deliver Fast
6. Respect People
7. Optimize the Whole

If you already follow Agile principles, there is a good chance that you will reflect on those principles and you already apply them in your Agile working environment.

So as you can see, Lean and Agile are overlapping in the software development process. They are not alternatives: if you are Agile you are Lean and sometimes vice-versa.(Figure 2-3).

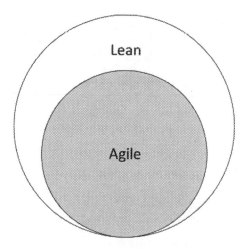

Figure 2-3. Lean vs. Agile

---

[1]http://www.poppendieck.com/

Agile Scrum Deep Dive

As I have mentioned before, Scrum methodology is one of the most popular if not *the* most popular way to implement Agile.

This methodology was developed by Ken Schwaber and Jeff Sutherland. The cornerstone of Scrum is described in the official Scrum Guide.[1]

The Scrum approach is to divide the project into smaller logical chunks (mini projects) and execute those in short iterations of ideally one to three weeks. Those iterations are called Sprints (Figure 3-1).

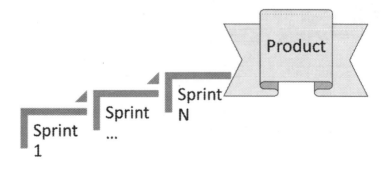

Figure 3-1. Scrum iterations(Sprints)

[1]http://www.scrumguides.org/

So instead of running a long marathon to an imaginary destination like we did in Waterfall, we divide the distance into short Sprints with a visible finish line. The shorter the Sprint duration the more visible the finish, and the easier it is to plan and predict the outcome and decide where we go next.

It is easier to detect "mistakes" when the team is coding the wrong stuff, assuming we have regular feedback from customer (or their proxy PO) to tell what the team delivered wrong—for example because of incomplete software requirements.

By doing so we achieve many advantages vs. the Waterfall model.

A – *Continuous improvement*: Since we run a complete software cycle in each iteration of design-develop-test, we improve from iteration to iteration.

B – *Transparency*: We get a lot of review points that allow us to see the final result, since the goal of each Sprint is to produce a complete functional code that we can demo, review, and ideally deploy to the customer at the end of each Sprint. (With classic Waterfall, even if we set **checkpoints**, they usually just allow us to see where we are with regard to the original master plan, which could become outdated)

C – *Early adoption*: As mentioned in point B. We are able to **deliver** at the end of each Sprint even if are not fully done. It makes early adoption possible.

D – *Embracing change*: Since software development is divided into chunks, after each chunk we get the opportunity to reflect and align whether we are going in right direction, and we get the opportunity to make changes.

The Scrum Team

Agile Scrum methodology implies a self-containing and self-managing team. Usually, we talk about teams of ten that will include the following roles. Developers, Scrum Master, Product Owner, Architect, Quality Engineer, and in some cases Technical Writer.

Team composition is based on the nature of the work and the current situation in your organization. However, the most important part is that the team will be self-governed. To get the best results, you should take the approach of dividing your company into smaller subcompanies.

Let's discuss all the roles in the team in more detail (Figure 3-2).

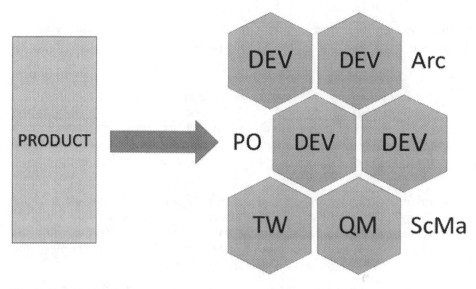

Figure 3-2. Team roles

The **Product Owner (PO)** collects requirements from customers (internal or external) and produces the requirements documents. The PO constantly **aligns with customers** and determines the **scope** of work and change in the scope, so the PO will get results from the Sprints. The PO is responsible for providing all the necessary product-related information required by the team and **providing requirements.**

The **Scrum Master (ScMa)** is the **servant-leader** of the team who helps the team to **deliver** based on requirements. The ScMa **organizes** the process and **moderates** the meetings that will enable the team to deliver. Also, the ScMa **provides statuses** to the PO or any stakeholders. The ScMa is in charge of resolution of any **block and impediments** the team faces. The ScMa shelters and **protects** the team from external teams and stakeholders.

▓ **Note**   The performance of the individual team members and other HR topics are not the ScMa's direct responsibility. There is another role Line Manager that is responsible for the performance of individual team members. Line Manager is direct manager for all the members of the Scrum team.

The **Architect (Arc)** is the technical lead in the team. Often, most of his or her time will be dedicated to guiding other team members, rather than individual tasks. The Architect creates/approves design, reviews code, and works in close sync with the ScMa and PO.

░ **Note**   Not every Scrum team has an Architect; however, at least one senior developer on the team should have profound expertise on technical aspects of the work.

The **Quality Manager (QM)** or Quality Engineer(QE) is the team member responsible for quality management of the product. The QM organizes the quality process in the team, educates the PO and ScMa on **quality best practices**, and provides quality requirements to the team based on feedback from the PO, industry standards, and best practices (Including performance, security, usability, accessibility etc.).

Developers (DEV) estimate and commit to the estimation on a Sprint basis. They constantly **improve the accuracy** of the estimation and self-improve from Sprint to Sprint without micromanagement from other roles and managers. Developers distribute between the different expert roles—for example performance, security, and user interface designer.

A **Technical Writer (TW)** writes supporting documentation for the project. This role can be centralized, since it is usually not required to have a full-time technical writer in the team. However, technical documentation also can be produced by any other role/roles in the team as an additional responsibility.

How Scope is Divided

There can be different naming conventions on how we can divide the project scope. Often any executable and prioritized parts of scope are called backlogs; however, the common naming convention in Scrum methodology is:

Epic ➤ User Story ➤ Task

When:

> *Epic:* something that doesn't have to fit into a Sprint. It can be broken down to several stories. Epic is how product owners divide requirements into logical groups. It can be executed over the duration of several Sprints.

> *Story:* something actionable and small enough to **fit in a Sprint**. It can be broken down to several tasks.

> *Tasks:* parts of a story that can be completed by a single team member. I recommend that a task should not exceed 18 hours of planned effort

For example:

We add to our travel agency website section where users will be able to exchange experience of their trips. This will be our Epic.

It will consist of many stories.

- *Story 0:* All sold trips will be available on the site.

- *Story 1*: User should be able to create a review for the trip she/he has purchased.

- *Story 2*: Site administrator will be able to validate the review before it will get published.

- *Story 3*: User can get likes from other users and have a rating.

- *Story 4*: Site administrator will be able to delegate moderation responsibilities to users with high ratings.

- ...

You see how Story has been split in a way that every story is encapsulated functionaly that can be deployed after completion. Also each story is small enough to be completed during one Sprint.

And the tasks, for example, for Story 0:

- *Task 1*: Create trips API where we can read data from the Agency DB (18 hours)

- *Task 2*: Create web page that will display all the content of trips API, with sorting and paging (12 hours)

- *Task 3*: Add Search by destination, hotel, country, city to the trips web page we created (14 hours)

- ....

Sprint Cycle and Meetings

Every Sprint should be dedicated to the execution of a certain user stories.

The team commits to complete those user stories according to **Done criteria**. (Done criteria will be explained later in the "Definition of Done" section of this chapter.)

There are certain meetings that are usually performed during one Sprint iteration—of course, a Scrum meeting that is executed on a daily basis and core meetings on a Sprint Level: Planning, Review, Retrospective and Backlog Grooming.

> Sprint (N) Planning ➤ Next Sprint (N+1) **backlog Grooming** ➤ Sprint (N) Review ➤ Sprint (N) Retrospective.

Figure 3-3 shows an example of a meeting cycle for a two-week Sprint. Of course, all those meetings are not set in stone and can be adjusted based on need.

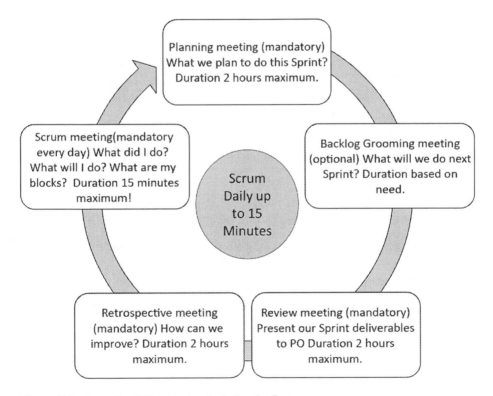

Figure 3-3. Example of Meeting details during the Sprint

Planning (mandatory) meeting: The team plans what user stories (backlogs) it will execute during the Sprint and breaks them into tasks. The team commits to completing those during the Sprint according to the Definition of Done (DoD).

Backlog grooming (optional) during execution of the Sprint N: The PO will introduce new backlogs if required and this meeting wil be an opportunity for the team **to ask questions** about backlogs for the next Sprint (N+1).

Sprint review (mandatory): The ScMa and the team present to the PO all the backlogs that were committed this Sprint, and status according to the DoD.

Retrospective (mandatory) team meeting: Team members discuss what went wrong, what went well, and if anything should be changed to improve team performance—also used as a meeting to release some steam. (Can be executed every second Sprint in case of short Sprints.)

Scrum meeting or **Stand-up** (mandatory): short daily meeting where team developers answer three questions: What was done since the last meeting? What are the blocks? What will I be doing next?

Even though some meetings are stated as optional and some as mandatory, try to understand the nature and purpose of the meeting and to determine meeting need use common sense in order not to create a waste and have unnecessary long meetings (rituals) without added value.

For example, if a team was not able to deliver during the Sprint and all backlogs will move to the next Sprint, backlogs grooming and backlogs introduction might not be required. From another side, **retrospective** might be a good idea to **determine what went wrong**.

Planning Process

The Planning meeting is the most critical meeting of the Sprint. The main goal of planning is to figure out to what user stories (backlogs) the team will commit during the current Sprint. If planning is not performed correctly (effort underestimated for example), the team will not be able to deliver what it commits to or will work extra hours to complete all the Sprint deliverables.

In case work is overestimated, the team always should have an additional backlog list it can take in case of available capacity. During planning, the team not only estimates but also breaks user stories into smaller tasks. It is possible to assign tasks to individuals, but also possible to keep it open for anyone to pick.

Task breakdown should be reasonably detailed. The task should be a **logical unit of work.**

▨ **Note** There are always some routine tasks that should be executed for different task categories. For example, if you developed a feature, you want to have a unit test for this feature, test case, automation, documentation, etc. So in some cases in order not to create too much clatter, instead of having a separate task for each activity they can be grouped all together. Create pre-templates that can be used for different types of tasks.

This will simplify the process of planning and tracking during the Sprint. It will be the executor's responsibility to include supporting tasks in the estimate.

You don't have to assign any task for the **routine work** of the technical writer, ScMa, QE, Architect, and PO. There are certain routine, role-relevant tasks that they have to execute and it is **the responsibility of those roles to manage their time and progress.** That is, unless there are some additional tasks that are not repetitive, for example, preparation of landscape for the ScMa, testing for the PO, development task for the QE, or a testing task for the technical writer.

It is not a good idea to have long and tedious planning meetings where people are bored and disengaged. So far, my favorite pattern in two-week Sprints is to have 30 minutes to 1 hour of planning. This can be achieved if user stories have owners assigned to them upfront, and those owners monitor those user stories and prepare a breakdown of tasks for the planning meeting. This can be quickly validated with the team and assigned during planning. (It doesn't mean that the owner of the user story has to execute it.)

Another process to speed up the planning is for the ScMa **not to monitor time assigned versus capacity**—each developer individually **calculates their time** and commits to a certain amount of tasks they are able to execute during the Sprint.

Definition of Done

Before the team starts implementing anything, it has to arrive at a certain agreement (DoD) on what steps are required to be executed in order to **consider work done**. This can be agreed among the QE, PO, and other relevant stakeholders. Of course, it is a living document and can be adjusted and modified if agreed by stakeholders. It is important not to overinflate this document because, if there too many conditions or the document is too complex, it will not work. **The less, the better.**

For example, DoD from one of my recent projects is shown in Figure 3-4:

- *1st column*: defines how tasks should be considered completed on the Sprint level

- *2nd column*: defines tasks that have to be complete for the previous Sprint. For example, we cannot create **test automation** prior to completion of development so this task only can be executed in the **next Sprint.**

- *3rd column*: is what you have to do in order to **release** everything you developed during all the Sprints into production.

On Sprint Level	On Sprint N + 1 Level	On Release Level
Unit tests	Documentation	Integration test executed (incidents resolved)
Static Code checks	Automation	
Security validated	Integration Test Case created	Product Standard Test Cases executed (incidents resolved)
Performance validated	Feedback from previous Sprint review integrated	Acceptance test executed (incidents resolved)
Down ported		
Code Inspection / Pair Programming		
Design Document updated		
Development completed		
Development tested		
QE tested with OK (incidents resolved)		

Figure 3-4. Definition of Done (DoD) example

Board

A board can be a software tool or physical board with post-its, where tasks after planning becomes posted and moved based on progress. Again, a board is just a tool. The board should not become work by itself, that is, nice progress on the board that **doesn't always translate to quality software and successful projects.**

Figure 3-5 shows a simple flow of tasks on the board.

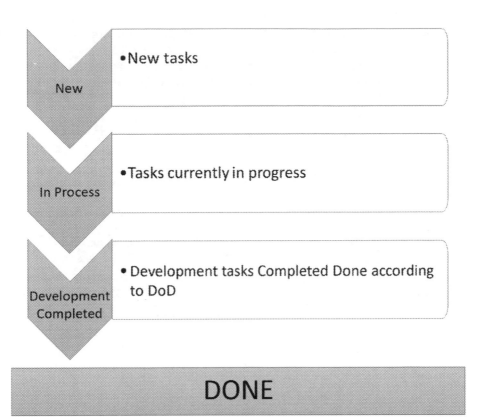

Figure 3-5. A simple flow of the task on the board

Team Rules

Sometimes it also makes sense to have a **certain set of rules** related to governing of the team. In case of making team rules, it is important to remember that the less is the better. Don't try to have rules for the sake of covering some hypothetical situation. Only the most necessary ones should be there, if at all—ideally less than ten.

The team determines if the rules are required; the ScMa just identifies the need and moderates the discussions. See a sample of team rules in Figure 3-6.

We have six hours in one day we can plan work for (estimate).
We monitor ourselves if we can do it or if we can't.
We measure our own accuracy (original vs. estimated) and improve every Sprint.
We monitor our own capacity during planning and Sprint execution.
We are true with ourselves.

Figure 3-6. Example of Team rules

Blocks and Impediments

The role of ScMa is to resolve blocks and impediments. So it is very critical for the ScMa to know about those. As well, the ScMa should be at the central hub of things that are going in the team and project; this allows being able to resolve different situation by having the **whole picture**.

To solve blocks and impediments, the ScMa should have the following resources: unbiased common sense, a general overview as being role-exposed to every aspect of the project, communication with team members, an external **network of experts**, and connection with external-to-team stakeholders.

If the ScMa is not able to solve a block/impediment, it is important to have a **predefined escalation process.**

Usually, the escalation process includes identifying **a few capable internal and external-to-team stakeholders** who have the capabilities of solving issues within the organization. It is very important for the ScMa to be **proactive** and to **prevent possible blocks before they occur.**

Velocity

Velocity is the magic word that is critical to any project manager. Basically, velocity is how much work we can execute in a certain time frame.

There are different ways to look at velocity, but no way is perfect. Let's look at several possibilities and possible challenges for each one of those.

1. Story points to measure velocity: This is the most common approach in Scrum. Story points are estimates of effort assigned to user stories based on the amount of work, complexity, uncertainty, and risk.

Eventually the team will learn how many story points it can take during a Sprint and it will be considered as team velocity. To measure the velocity, average of the last three Sprints can be used.

However there are a few problems with it:

For a team to master how to determine story points in a way that makes sense can be tricky.

Plus, each team will use their own scale of measurement to calculate the story points. As a result, often stakeholders get confused and judgmental when team A velocity is 2,000 story points but team B is 50,000 per Sprint, but in reality team A is more productive.

In addition, usually capacity is calculated in hours and stakeholders operate with PDs (Person days) and hours, so conversion between story points and hours can become a pain point for the ScMa and PO when is required to produce reporting.

Also in cases when tasks in the team are not repetitive, it might be very challenging to operate with such metrics to get accurate velocity.

2. Velocity in hours on task level: Measure and estimate velocity by the level of hours per tasks and derive from this team velocity on a Sprint level.

This can be derived also from adding the estimates of the tasks that have been completed or from the actual time that it took to execute those tasks

Although this may look like the most accurate way of getting the velocity, in reality it could be the contrary. A lot of overhead for the ScMa and a lot of misleading data will be provided and included in calculations.

Often team members are affected by their peers when doing planning estimates, and often the time entered for execution of the tasks also can be affected because of social/peer pressure (For this reason story points can provide more accurate result during planning).

3. High-level velocity by expert: rough estimates from senior developers/ architect of the work team is capable to complete in a Sprint. A most experienced and skilled developer, by looking at the team as a whole and learning from the historical perspective, is able to determine how much can be achieved during one Sprint and if team improves.

This approach is holistic and based on one individual who knows best and not on any particular mesurments. The problems with this approach are:

- It is not always possible to find such a talented individual in the team.

- This individual becomes a bottleneck for the team. The team will lose its velocity estimator (benchmark) once she/he is gone.

- This spoon feeding approach doesn't contribute to development of the team, even if it gives good results in some cases.

Tools

There are different tools on the market for project management besides the white board with stickers. For example: Jira, Trello, Microsoft project, or even Excel.

However, usage of any tool doesn't guarantee you success. In the case of remote teams, project managing software can become handy, but with a local team the whiteboard can be just fine.

Use tools only when they simplify the process and don't make it more complex. Shape up the process and introduce tools later if there is a clear benefit out of them.

To use something digital, a simple wiki page with statuses and a whiteboard with post-its can be sufficient. Fancy tools are not something that drives the process; it is important not to become a servant of the tool!

Often Scrum execution is monitored with a burndown chart, which is basically a visualization of the current Sprint tasks time estimates vs. what was completed so far vs. The time remaining. Figure 3-7 is a sample of a burndown chart taken from the Jira tool. In this burndown chart, the blue line indicates amount of hours spent by developers during the Sprint and the green line indicates burndown of the backlog. The red line is just a marker that indicates ideal burndown progress.

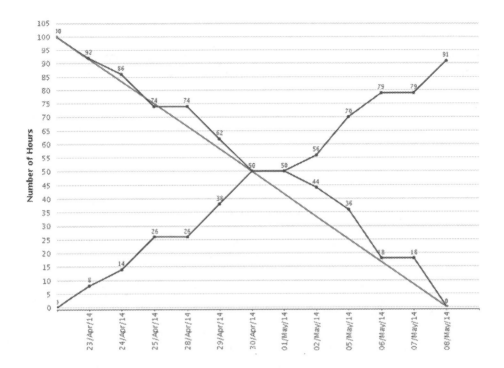

Figure 3-7. Burndown chart taken from the Jira tool

This burndown describes a Sprint when estimates were accurate and all tasks have been executed.

If the estimates are realistic, data is up to date, and everybody is logging their time and progress accurately, this chart might add value. But there are too many ifs...

From my practice, having a burndown chart and logging time is not always required. I believe that if the developer just commits to some tasks during a Sprint, it is his/her responsibility to understand what capacity he/she has and if a developer can do it (no micromanagement). In this case it is the developer's responsibility to highlight any issues with the Sprint commitments.

Important to Always Keep in Mind

Scrum is based on controlled iterations—Sprints, where a team gets better from iteration to iteration and will have a control point at the end of each iteration. Three main factors that form the basis of Scrum methodology success are: transparency, inspection, and adaptation.

However, despite that we have talked mainly about processes in this chapter, it is important to reflect that Scrum is team-centric methodology applied to self-organized teams.

It is most successful when each team member commits to achieving the goal of the Sprint for the whole team.

It takes many different technical and soft skills, personalities, and talents for the team to be successful, and Scrum team members should respect each other in order to have a successful team.

Scrum is like a wine: it should get better with time, but if not done correctly it will become vinegar.

Agile Scrum methodology methods and techniques are intended to support the Agile principles of:

- Individuals and interaction over processes and tools
- Working software over comprehensive documentation
- Customer collaboration over contract negotiation
- Responding to change over following a plan

Methodology is a tool that is here to help. Creating beautiful burndowns and using the latest buzz words, acronyms, and techniques is not the goal. The goal is to deliver great software that the customer actually wants and needs; at the highest quality in the most optimal way; in the most motivating, performant, and dynamic work environment. The key is a self-governing, cross-functional team that improves from iteration to iteration and that is fun to be a member of.

Religiously following different methods and techniques is not the goal. Always start simple. On http://scrumyes.com/ I am describing a simplified version of Agile Scrum implementation to facilitate initial Scrum adoption.

Scrum Master: What It's All About

The Scrum Master (ScMa) is a servant-leader who monitors and improves the processes of Agile Scrum Methodology. The ScMa has no authority like a Line Manager who can hire and fire, and often controls salaries and bonus distribution. Also the ScMa has no authority like the Product Owner (PO), who has authority and accountability over the product and is dictating to the team what the product should be like.

So in this context, the ScMa really has no defined authority and it is all about soft power.

The role can be challenging and not satisfying, since in case of success ScMa will almost never get any credit from the team and in case of failure might be the first one to be blamed.

When the PO is accountable for the product, the ScMa has no defined part of the responsibility other than overall processes but will, however, be accountable for almost everything, since processes are set up for every part of the project. From this prospective, the ScMa role can be one of the most challenging on the Scrum team.

© Ilya Bibik 2018

I. Bibik, *How to Kill the Scrum Monster*, https://doi.org/10.1007/978-1-4842-3691-8_4

Influence Without Authority

The traditional role of project manager (PM) in the Scrum team gets divided between the PO and ScMa, when the ScMa is in charge **for process** and the PO for **product requirements**. However, when the PO still has some level of authority with regard to the product, the ScMa has it more challenging since ScMa has no authority at all and has to act in a way of soft power.

This requires having a certain amount of support from the team because, if in certain situations the ScMa has to take action on certain aspects and if there is a disconnect between the team and the ScMa, it can lead to a situation that will make everyday operations challenging.

In some cases, unacceptance (hostility) can unite the team against the ScMa and make the work process almost impossible.

For example: If there is a junior ScMa with a relatively senior team, changes the ScMa is trying to push might not be accepted by the team, and can be rejected and create a disconnect between the team and the ScMa.

One of the very challenging aspects of the ScMa role is to gain acceptance of the team.

Since the ScMa doesn't have manager authority, there are no other tools besides persuasion to lead team members, and it is very difficult to have every member of your team on board with you and to deliver the right message to them.

The ScMa is an advocate of continuous improvement and that means change, and change usually triggers resistance to change.

On top of it, team member's are typically busy and additional load for improvement and changes from the ScMa often might not be adopted or even understood.

The ScMa has to show the team that the ScMa is on their side and is just another team member. However, it is not always possible to gain respect and build relations with all the team members; in this case, it is just important to maintain neutral status and involve the Line Manager for problem resolution.

Scrum Master Admin Work Trap

If you already execute the ScMa role and all you do is keep the Admin tasks and fill your time only with those, you are in the wrong place. Admin tasks can be very disruptive but they are just a tiny fraction of your role responsibilities. Your goal is to **deliver software** and not to produce graphs, boards, excels, and organize fancy meetings using fancy terminology. Administrative overkill that compensates for the ScMa's feeling of being useless is very disruptive to the team. It is better to do nothing and just observe the dynamics and step in when required rather than create unnecessary bureaucracy and distract the team to justify role existence, in case the ScMa doesn't know any better.

Combining Other Roles with the Scrum Master Role

It could be that in your organization the ScMa role is not considered a full-time role and is combined with other roles.

Let's discuss a few possible combinations and what could be the issues.

Scrum Master/Developer

It makes sense for the ScMa to have developer background but does not necessarily make sense for the ScMa to be a developer in the team. The reason is that the ScMa role **workload is not determined**, so there is an issue for the ScMa to commit to tasks during the Sprint—especially during short Sprints, since the ScMa role can take 100% of capacity. Another problem is upskilling—if the team has to ramp up on new technologies, the ScMa might not get the same opportunity as the rest of the developers due to the load of work from the ScMa role. Also, the role of ScMa is very disruptive and doesn't always provide the opportunity or time frame to ramp up and get hands-on experience for a sufficient period of time. For this reason, the dev role will work best when there are dev tasks that are not part of the Sprints, for example, writing a prototype for next release during the first release or writing automation scripts for the whole project but not on a Sprint basis.

Scrum Master/Quality

This combination might have the same issues as the combination with developer role (commitment on Sprint level and learning curve). However, the learning curve might be less steep than in the dev role so it might work better, especially in case there is an additional quality expert on the team and the ScMa contributes when possible without being the bottleneck.

Scrum Master/Line Manager

This might be a sweet spot for the ScMa, since the role changes from no authority into actual authority. This can work, but it depends totally on the personality of the ScMa. Will this individual hold the team hostage or be able to overcome the micromanagement tendency and deliver the best of both roles?

Note Dictatorship also can be positive but really depends on the dictator. It's really against Agile principles to have a dictator in a self-organized team, but still can work in case of a good dictator and a team that actually needs it.

Scrum Master/Product Owner/Business Analyst

The PO is different from organization to organization: sometimes the PO on the team is just the team member who brings requirements to the team and not the one who defines them. We can call this PO/Business Analyst. Sometime the PO can define requirements by himself. So I don't think it will work for the ScMa to have both roles of ScMa and PO; however, I definitely see that the ScMa on the team can be PO/Business Analyst. Again it all depends on the complexity of the project and particular situation. General practice in the industry doesn't recommend merging those two roles, due to potential conflict of interest.

Note What we haven't discussed here are different expert roles that might be mandatory in your organization, such as security, performance, automation, usability, etc. Some of those also can be on the ScMa's plate, especially if expert deliverables are spread over the duration of the project and don't have hard commitments on a Sprint level.

Perceptions, Personalities, and Conditions

So far we discussed different methodologies and ScMa roles and adaptations; however, what makes it really **difficult is the people.** Each team member is an individual persona with her/his own set of perceptions, different background, and different level of personal and career development. So, first of all, no team will be perfect; there will always be team members that you might not be happy with, as well as team members that might not be happy with you as the ScMa. This can be justified or unjustified, since it's all a matter of individual perceptions. The ScMa cannot always win a popularity contest in the team, not that ScMa necessarily has to be popular (it does help, however).

There is a common set of personalities you might get in your team: The diva; the timid, insecurity compensator; the insecure; the loud and useless; the individualist; the overachiever; the kid; the amazing; etc.

On top of it there are different situations that are not dependent on perceptions but on certain deviations. The ScMa should be familiar with the most common conditions of Asperger's syndrome, autism, ADD, psychopaths, narcissists, etc.

For the ScMa to able to fulfill his/her role effectively requires three main qualities: to be mature, self-aware, and emotionally intelligent.

Commitment of Scrum Master to Additional Tasks

Often it is expected of the ScMa to contribute to development or other tasks, assuming ScMa is not a role that consumes all the capacity of the team member, for example, 50%/50%. The problem with it is that sometimes the role will take 100% of the time with overtime but in some cases 30% to 40%, and it is very difficult to predict what direction a Sprint will go with regard to ScMa involvement. The magic formula is not to commit to productive tasks on a Sprint level. There are usually topics that are executed on the whole project level. For example, in the case of development the ScMa can work on backlogs that are not committed for the current Sprint, or on general topics that apply to the project as a whole such as test automation, performance, test data, quality management, etc. As well, the ScMa can be the team expert on some topics like security, performance, UI, etc. That don't have hard commitments on a Sprint level.

It is important for the ScMa to be transparent with the team on what he is doing, since often the ScMa role and duties are not clear within the team, and the ScMa contribution and deliverable are not always visible to team members.

However, in the case of a mature self-driven team, the ScMa role can be less demanding and in this case, the ScMa can actually commit on a Sprint level.

Scrum Master Technical Skills

There is a good chance that the ScMa is coming from a technical background. So if the team is working in a technical domain where the ScMa has expertise, there should be no issue to be able to get a good understanding on topics team is working on. However, if the team is changing technologies and projects, the ScMa will have difficulty to ramp up on the new topics since the nature of this role is a constant disruption that makes it difficult to concentrate on same thing for long period of time and master new topics.

Estimating and Monitoring Your Team

Estimations are often not accurate unless the work is really repetitive.

For this reason, if you as the ScMa feel trapped in number games and monitoring without seeing any benefit, maybe the hours counting can just be dropped.

If the Sprint is short enough, let's say two weeks, instead of matching capacity to task estimation, a simple way out can be that developers will pick up certain backlogs and commit to them during planning and it will be the developer's responsibility to track the time and improve in the next Sprint iterations. This way all the tasks are preassigned and there is no tracking of time on the Sprint level; as well, you are not putting anyone in the spotlight for how much time it takes them to execute certain tasks. Of course, you can claim that by not measuring the individual time you are missing topics such as velocity calculation, tracking of Sprint progress, and tracking improvement. However, my argument is that the team is a unit, so if you do want to track time, track on the team level and measure velocity and improvement on the team level.

Also with regard to Sprint execution progress, if your Sprint does not exceed the duration of two weeks, individual time tracking does not add much value. In my experience a holistic approach works much better.

Unfortunately, sometimes management will push to get the numbers in order to satisfy their reporting instincts and then you will not necessarily have a choice.

Accepting Change by the Team

When change is imposed on a teams or individuals, both individuals and teams usually resist the change and the ScMa who has to deal with it and roll out the change.

There are different ways to deal with change resistance. Before changing anything, observe the existing process you plan to change and what are frustrating points/difficulties the team is experiencing right now.

Explain to the team the issue they are having, making sure the team understands the problem and root cause.

After having a team on board collect feedback, process it and roll out the solution.

As a rule of thumb, every change should be easy to implement, easy to understand, and should feel natural. Also, don't implement too many changes for each iteration—less is better.

But there is not always time for it, as well. Not every topic makes sense to open for discussion, so the ScMa should act based on the situation.

To overcome resistance, the changes should be explained and make sense and if not accepted or not understood, postponed or dismissed.

However, some changes will need to be enforced and might create a conflict situation between the ScMa and some of the team members.

It is important to identify when it makes sense to use some external-to-the-team resource to enforce the change, in order not to destroy the relationship of the ScMa and the team.

For example: Let's say an organization is rolling out migration from Waterfall to Agile Scrum, and a new ScMa was hired. The team is a senior team that resists change. In a case where the ScMa rolls out the process, the team might become dysfunctional in the future. However, if a change is a rollout by higher management and the ScMa is introduced as an Agile PM who has Scrum experience and will help team to overcome the difficult transformation times, then the ScMa will be perceived as help and not as an imposer.

Build Scrum Master Confidence

When you run the role of ScMa your confidence can be often challenged. It is very difficult to be a leader without authority, and you can easily become a shooting target to your team and to players external to the team. Having elephant skin helps but no matter how thick your skin is, it can be penetrated; the more penetrations your get, the more your confidence can be shaken.

However, in this case, remember this: "Knowledge builds confidence, and confidence creates mastery." Start training a lot. The more you read and hear about the process the more confident you become. Books, Quora questions, wiki, podcasts, YouTube—there are so many sources of information. Reach out to other ScMa's; understand the challenges. Use your manager to talk out your issues and to look for solutions; as well, an ScMa should build a support system that can include some peers and managers who will provide support, advice, and assistance during challenging periods.

Scrum Master = Project Manager?

I find the statement that the ScMa is not a PM to be a somewhat controversial point. So just let's clarify the difference:

- Scrum Master works on process
- Project manager works on the project

Many people think that the ScMa is not a PM, even though they share some responsibilities when some part of those responsibilities are on the PO, and the ScMa should be a servant-leader who concentrates on the process and continuous improvement.

However, no matter what those articles say, the eventual role of the ScMa, as well as every other team member, is also to deliver the project.

I believe that the ScMa role not only facilitates the process and constantly improves it, resolving blocks and impediments, but also makes sure that teams deliver. All this process isn't worth much if we continuously improve but fail to deliver. Even if the process is great; however, there is always something that can fall through the cracks.

The ScMa together with the PO replace the conventional PM, so if they will not execute essential parts of the PM role, then who will? Working with stakeholders, they mitigate expectations, predict risks, catch things that get overlooked, and oversee all the project and its timelines and not just one iteration. So maybe the ScMa is not a PM from the classical point of view. However, I believe that the ScMa receives different pieces of a puzzle and tries to help assemble it in a way that satisfies the customer. Maybe this is done by looking more at the process than on the project, but the goal is the same: the team has to deliver.

So is the ScMa a PM? I don't know really and I don't care. Just make it happen and put in any title. Some compare ScMa role to that of a sheepdog but I believe the best name/title that describes the ScMa role is an "lubricant" or "oil." The role of the ScMa is to lubricate everything in order for the team to be able to reach its maximum potential. The lubricant is something not visible, but without it nothing works or even if it does work for some time, eventually the mechanism wears out very fast.

To conclude: the ScMa role is not a simple role. It takes a lot to be able to influence without authority and to be a servant-leader of the team. The ScMa is the one responsible for promoting and supporting Scrum methodology adaptation in the team. The ScMa is a servant-leader for the Scrum team at the same time the ScMa provides service to the PO to enable the PO to execute his/her role in an optimal way. ScMa optimizes the process in the team to help the team to achieve the most value, and protects his/her team members from themselves and from external interruptions.

Team Dynamics

It is essential to be aware of what is going on with his team dynamics, and it helps to have at least a slight clue on how to describe the team stages. I recommend getting familiar with Tuckman's Stages of Group Development.[1] There are four stages: Forming, Storming, Norming, and Performing.

- **Forming.** This is the initial stage after formation of the team. The team members try to be accepted by their peers. With certain exceptions, team members try to avoid conflicts and concentrate on organization of the team and processes. Team members try to collect information and feedback about each other, about future tasks and the best way to approach those tasks. This is not a very productive stage, where all the team members try to stay in their initial comfort zone and the team feels comfortable to be in this stage as long as it can. However, avoidance of conflict and the umbrella of initial forming processes that justify nonproductivity usually mean that not much will get done at this stage.

- **Storming.** After the initial comfortable stage of forming, the less conformist stage of storming starts and conflicts and disagreements usually start. Some of the Scrum team members will be involved in minor conflicts. Usually the

---

[1] B. W. Tuckman, "Developmental Sequence in Small Groups," *Psychological Bulletin*, 63(6), 384-399, 1965.

I. Bibik, *How to Kill the Scrum Monster*, https://doi.org/10.1007/978-1-4842-3691-8_5

team will try to suppress those conflicts in order to move forward; however, the initial conflicts will be there under the carpet and ready to burst. At this stage team members will feel that they are winning or losing; so clear rules and process, and involvement of different Scrum team roles as well as Line Manager will be required in order to overcome those situations. At the same time, not all team members will be comfortable moving into the storming stage, and some will still remain in the comfortable Forming stage for a longer duration of time.

- **Norming.** After the storm of the Storming stage, everything stabilizes and certain norms are established in the team. It is clear who in the team is doing what and how, and the team understands strengths and weaknesses of team members and what can be expected from them. Roles and responsibilities are clear to all the team members.

- Team members listen to each other and support each other. Basically, at this stage the team starts to operate as a unit for the first time. The team spent effort to be in the norming stage and will be very defensive in case some external-to-the-team forces try to influence or micromanage team dynamics, and will bring the team back to the Storming stage. The team is performing at this stage and is able to deliver.

- **Performing.** This is the final stage and the desired stage for every Scrum team. Everyone knows and trusts each other and each team member is comfortable to work together. The trust level allows each team member to work individually on the common goal. Each team member will assist other team members and other roles to achieve the common goal, and this will happen without saying or highlighting this to other team members. Team members will identify themselves as having high-level loyalty to the group and group members. The group will be equally task oriented and people oriented. Basically, in my view the goal of Scrum methodology being team-centered methodology is to bring the team into the Performing stage.

Why should you get familiar with all the stages other than curiosity? First of all the ScMa, Line Manager, and Product Owner (PO) should understand the Performing and Storming stages and be aware that during the early stages, the team most likely will be not very performant and they should manage the expectations of the stakeholders accordingly.

As well, the ScMa and other team roles that are coaching the team should recognize team Norming and Storming stages, since during this time it is very important to help bring the team to an established set of rules, values, and the middle ground in order for the team to operate and become more efficient.

Without the ScMa or any other leaders in the team, the team might not be operational and will not reach the next stages. Conflict situations will become unbearable and make the team environment totally acidic.

Once the rules and values of the team are established, the team can self-regulate and will reach the Norming and Performing stages.

▨ **Note**   Sometimes regression in a team can happen, and sometimes different parts of teams can be in different stages. For example, senior team members may achieve Norming and Performing stages in a subgroup relatively fast, while more junior team members may remain in the Storming or Forming stage for a longer period of time.

Different stages in the team are achieved by experiencing self-improvements during Sprint iterations and also partly because of the healthy visible and invisible conflicts. The team has to make sure that conflicts, even when they are healthy, don't become destructive and will not interfere with team-forming dynamics.

Relationships Between Roles in the Team

Another factor critical to team success is relationships between different roles in the team.

First of all, you need two to tango. A relationship cannot be sustained only by one side. So it is a critical role of the Line Manager (or anyone who assembles the team originally) to make sure that healthy working relationships between key roles are established. Just having top performer who cannot work well with each other can be less effective sometimes than having less performant individuals who integrate well in the team as a unit.

In order for a team to be successful, there are many personalities and many skill sets required to be arranged correctly together. Building a team is like assembling a puzzle that has never been assembled before.

Being a team player is obviously the most critical skill that ensures an individual is able to contribute in the team environment, will not be disruptive, and eventually will develop working relationships with other team members.

Scrum Master–Product Owner

The ScMa and PO relationship is the most critical relationship in the team; there should be 100% trust and understanding between the two roles. Any clashes between the two will have a very negative impact on team performance and development. If there is a problem between those two roles, the Line Managers's role is to make necessary adjustments as fast as possible.

Architect–Product Owner/Architect–Scrum Master

The Architect–PO/Architect–ScMa relationship are also very critical relationships in the team. Often the Architect will be the one who translates the requirements from the PO into an executable design, so any communication problems between PO and Architect can impose a major risk to the project. Also, the execution level ScMa should work closely with the Architect to make the planning and dev process as smooth and effective as possible.

Scrum Master–Quality Manager

The ScMa-QM (Quality Manager) relationship is also important, since there are many processes that are related to quality management in the team and the ScMa role is to improve and optimize the processes. The ScMa usually should be tightly engaged with the quality expert in the team.

Architect–Developers

The Architect is technical lead and also sometimes coach for the other developers in the team. This is another very important relationship for the success of the project. It is important that the ScMa ensures communication flow and, in case of any issue, to mediate between the Architect and development using either interpersonal skills or enabling processes in place that make the communication possible.

For example, if developers feel intimidated by Architect criticism, the ScMa can set up code review sessions where the ScMa will be the moderator and will insure a smooth process of the code review. Sometimes formalizing the process can be an effective tool that will eliminate negative emotions and stress from the feedback provided.

Another issue could be fear of asking questions by the team to the Architect. Formalizing the process and using tools such as email or question board and question time slots can help to overcome negative emotions, thus avoiding the Architect getting irritated from constant interruptions.

Scrum Master–Developers

Many people will have different personalities. Since there can be four to five developers in the team, it could be challenging for the ScMa to have perfect relationships with everyone in the team. However, since the personalities in the team might not necessarily have a perfect click with each other, it is critical for the ScMa and Line Manager to help build a workable relationship structure in the team. Using personal communication skills and team building activities is required.

Product Owner–Team

The PO should be part of the team and not be isolated. The PO should not give the team a feeling of being superior and not one of the team members. The PO should be aware of what is going on in the team but at the same time should not try to micromanage other roles. The PO should be located together with all the team members, participate in team activities, and be transparent to the team about his/her workload.

If the PO self-isolates and becomes unapproachable, it will be a path to team failure and make the team environment very toxic.

Technical Writer–Team

Despite documentation being a less important part of Agile development, there still might be a separate role of technical writer. Technical writers are not always technical, and it will be difficult for a technical writer to fit into the dynamics of the team simply due to not understanding the realities of the process. For the role of technical writer it is critical to have a working relationship with the PO. Since the PO is the one who has a final vision of what is delivered and why, eventually the PO's understanding of the deliverables should be reflected in the documentation. As well, for a technical writer it is useful to build a working relationship with the Quality Manager (QM) in the team, since both roles' work is following developers' deliverables in a similar way.

▓ **Note** Since the roles of Architect, PO, ScMa, and QM are unique in the team, it can occur that certain individuals will feel defensive within their role execution. For example, the QM can feel that the ScMa is overstepping into the QM's responsibilities by optimizing the quality processes. Or the PO will try to micromanage project execution and will try to overstep team self-organizing dynamics and ScMa responsibilities. It is important for the Line Manager to get involved in such situations and coach the main roles into acceptable modes of operation.

External-to-Team Communications

It is very important to define the correct communication channels between the team and external stakeholders. If those relationships are not defined correctly, it can be a cause of major levels of stress and capacity lost in the team.

Team–Line Manager

Every team member is supervised by an Line Manager; however, the ScMa role should have a close, trust-based relationship with the Line Manager in order to be able to solve issues related to the team. Often Line Managers view their ScMa's as their "lieutenants" in the team.

Team–Program

In big organizations, development processes are often executed under some program that is driving based on timeline, landscape, and quality standards. Usually the team members who have to coordinate with the program are Quality for the quality standards, ScMa/PO for timelines and landscapes, and the Architect for central architecture guidelines.

Team–Stakeholders

Usually there are many stakeholders on each project. And, as per human nature, many of them will assume that they know better and might try to contact team members directly. It is also possible that team members themselves will try to bypass the communication channels established in the team for convenience reasons or for reason of individual selfish gains.

It is important to establish that external communications will always go throw the defined channels—for example, to go to the PO for requirements and the ScMa for process-relevant topics. Situations when the Chief PO or even the customer will change the requirements directly with developers, bypassing the

PO, can create major problems in the long run. In addition, if other teams try to use team resources in an unauthorized manner, this should be monitored and become part of the backlog rolled out by the PO if it requires substantial effort from team members. It is the responsibility of the ScMa to protect the team from distractions and to identify those situations, and each team member to report when it happens.

Note The purpose is not to eliminate team members from being exposed to external stakeholder or from developing networking with other team members; it is quite the contrary: team members should be exposed as much as possible to the stakeholders. The purpose is to illuminate the misalignments during project execution where there are few hubs of information and decision-making that will contribute to project failure in the long run, and when capacity lost is not accounted for.

Overall responsibility of the ScMa is to protect the team and individual team members from attacks from sources external to the team. It is the responsibility of the ScMa to be able to transform the attacks into constructive feedback, in order to avoid damage to the individual and to team dynamics in general. Of course in case something was done in the wrong way, it should be communicated and addressed, but it should be done in a constructive way and the ScMa should ensure that.

Conflict/Problems Resolutions

Let's talk more about conflicts, conflicts are not something that can be totally avoided and often conflicts and their resolution become a huge part of the ScMa role.

Sometimes there are almost no conflicts in the team. If this is your current situation, stick to this team and this role as long as you can no matter how much work you are getting and if your pay is not great.

Unfortunately, or in some cases fortunately, it is not always the case.

Usually, most of the conflicts are created by managers who assemble the team. They do not do it on purpose; it is just very difficult to understand if you combine certain people together how it will work.

The divorce rate is more than 50% in North America; what do you expect from a team of ten? If we took divorce rate as a measurement, then a team of ten is guaranteed to get a divorce.

But on the team, you can't ask some of the team members to sleep on the couch in the living room or go back to their parents' house. So the team, and the ScMa in particular, have to deal with conflicts and prevent them whenever required. This is a very substantial and very important invisible part of ScMa role responsibilities.

I identify four types of conflicts:

- **Type 1**—*The pure evil (political games)*: Power and politics are especially common in a big organization. It can be a conflict among managers, stakeholders, etc. When someone opens a destructive campaign against someone else for whatever reason, those conflicts can be devastating to the team and to anyone who tries to resolve them. It really hurts the company as well. Line management should be able to identify and prevent those. (Often they will not be able to.) There is no good way out of most of the evil conflicts other than running away by looking for new opportunities on the market.

  This type of conflict is always bad.

- **Type 2**—*Instinctual drives (human nature)*: This happens when an individual or individuals are not able to control their ego and operate purely on instincts and emotions. Any individual can get into emotion-driven mode; however, for some individuals their instinctual drives are dominant and cannot be controlled by their super ego or rationalism.

- Usually, the politically correct term for it is "not a team player." Line management should take care of this type of conflict by mentoring or removing the individual from the team. In case an Line Manager fails to deal with such individuals, productivity and development of the team as a whole will be affected.

- Another situation of this type of conflict sometimes is when one individual rejects another one on an emotional level. There is no particular reason: it's just that some individuals do not tolerate each other; sometimes they can provide an explanation for it but often this explanation just attempts to rationalize their deep emotions.

- Very often some team members will get into an argument just to try to prove that they're right and others are wrong. This situation can be very counterproductive.

Often it is difficult to handle such a case, since it can always be argued that a person has his opinion and the right to be heard and provide the arguments. As a result, attempts to moderate such situations can be interpreted as dictatorship.

For example, this might come up during retrospective meetings since it is relatively easy to come up with ideas for change and improvement when you don't really mean it but try to prove yourself right. Very often those counterproductive arguments destroy the purpose of meetings and discussions, and should be suppressed by the ScMa; otherwise the team will lose control and motivation.

This type of conflict is always bad.

- **Type 3**—*Miscommunication conflict:* When some messages are interpreted in the wrong way. It can get any shape and form. This conflict is unnecessary. Communication helps to resolve it; it is the role of the ScMa to enable the communication channel between the individuals.

- *This conflict is always bad but often simple to resolve.*
- **Type 4**—*The healthy conflict:* Usually, this is related to simple disagreement between team members for genuin reasons, and this type of conflict is analyzed in most conflict management books and papers.

This type of conflict is not always bad, and a resolution of this conflict will be discussed further.

Despite the negative nature of the conflict, a team in which everyone always agrees most likely will not be a very high-performance team and will not improve. You need brainstorm and use different opinions to succeed.

ScMa and Line Manager in the background has a big role in conflict resolutions in the team and both should know how to handle conflicts.

It is important for the team to establish a value that all the team members will be heard and that each team member should be able to adjust their ego, personal agenda, and emotions and be part of the team.

Unfortunately, not everyone is capable of suppressing their ego and emotions. At this stage, the art of conflict moderation begins.

Techniques of solving conflicts are standard everywhere; it doesn't matter if it is an Agile environment or not.

- *COLLABORATE (Win–Win)*: In this case, the ScMa/Line Manager can serve as facilitator rather than an active part of the solution. The input of both sides can be accommodated. This is the ideal situation: win–win.

- *COMPROMISE (Lose–Lose)*: In this case, both sides should agree to disagree but the show must go on, and both sides understand it. The ScMa/Line Manager might be heavily involved as intermediate in this type of issue.

- *FORCE (Win–Lose)*: Ideally, forcing is compliance to rules but such rules do not always exist. In this case, the ScMa should try not to be the enforcer but to use someone else with a less critical communication role or even external to the team. This way of dealing with conflict can escalate eventually to more conflicts; however, it could be the only way sometimes. It can result in using Line Manager or PO authority to force one of the sides to work in a certain way.

- *SMOOTH or ACCOMMODATE (Make it slide)*: The ScMa can do it if she/he has good communication skills, by smoothing the situation between the conflict sides on an individual basis. Smoothing most likely will pop up at a later stage. However, the ScMa should know when to pick her/his battles and this technique might have it's benefits.

- *WITHDRAW (Do nothing)*: This also can happen, especially when both sides are wrong. So the ScMa/Line Manager might closely observe the situation without putting her/himself on the line. In this case, an opportunity to solve the conflict might come with time.

- *LEAD the conflict (Take a side)*: Sometimes it makes sense for ScMa to take a side in a conflict and lead it, in order to control the situation and minimize damage.

Conflicts can be healthy when they promote constructive discussions. It is important that the resolution of conflicts is encouraged, and an environment is created where team members express their opinions and concerns with each other and about the project, and eventually agree on things, using common sense and reason instead of argument for the sake of argument and emotions as reasoning.

However, despite the possible positive outcome of the conflict, at the same time conflicting situations can severely reduce team productivity and it is very important to address the situation and keep it under control.

Due to the nature of Agile and because of decentralization and the pressure of working in short iterations, Agile can increase the number of conflicts in the team compared with the Waterfall model. This makes the ScMa's and Line Managers ability to resolve conflicts critical for team productivity and dynamics.

From another side, fear of conflict in a Scrum team is not always a good sign for the team. Lack of conflict can mean team apathy.

These are some additional readings I recommend on the topic:

- *The Five Dysfunctions of a Team: A Leadership Fable* (Jossey-Bass, 2002) by Patrick Lencioni. The author names "fear of conflict" as one of the team dysfunctions.

- "13 Steps for Navigating Conflict Effectively" is an article by Carl Robinson (*http://leadershipconsulting. com/13-steps-navigating-conflict-effectively*). The main message is that most people wait until contentious issues escalate and become a bigger problem before attempting to deal with them—conflict avoidance.

- "Coaching Through Conflict: Effective Communication Strategies" is an article by Ryan Hedstrom (*http:// www.appliedsportpsych.org/resources/ resources-for-coaches/coaching-through-conflict-effective-communication-strategies/*). Although this material is intended for sports coaches, I do find a lot of similarities between the sports coach and especially Scrum Master roles, and this material is definitely a good read.

Scrum Master as Part of Conflict

So far we discussed the conflicts on the level where the ScMa is not part of them; however, in an active role the ScMa can be more often directly involved in the conflicting situation.

Often when the ScMa is part of conflict, it doesn't necessarily mean that particular individual in the role of ScMa generates conflict. It can mean that the role of ScMa is more exposed to conflict situations, and those conflict situations should be solved with regular means of conflict resolution.

▓ **Note** The ScMa works with team dynamics, team conflicts and promotes changes and improvements, and as a result often the ScMa itself can be part of the conflict. However Line Manger also deals with conflicts but has actual authority that helps Line manager to be less exposed to be part of a conflict.

Conflict Bottom Line

Conflict, if unmoderated, can damage a team. The ScMa's and Line manager responsibility is to manage conflict; however, each person has different tools and has a set of soft skills that best work for him/her.

Advice for conflict moderators - yes it is good to get familiar with different papers and techniques of conflict resolution, but each conflict moderator should do what she is good at. As well, each situation is different and there is no tool to fix it all, so follow your gut feeling. Just don't get discouraged, and don't keep conflicts in the team unattended. Advice for of any other team member in the conflict situation: be self-aware and understand your strengths, weakness, and emotions. Use reasoning and not emotions. Give yourself 24 hours before reacting, especially in cases when emotions are involved. Respect whoever that tries to help you to moderate conflict it is not an easy task.

Key Takeaways

Despite the fact that I have used word agile starting with capital letter in this book it is important to remember that "agile" is not a noun, it is an adjective. However, industry often creates a monster from a good and relatively simple concept. Sometimes different individuals and companies try to take advantage of the trend by adding unnecessary content and services that concentrate more on methodology and additional techniques rather than on core values.

Core values of the Agile Manifesto are:

- Individuals and interaction over processes and tools

- Working software over comprehensive documentation

- Customer collaboration over contract negotiation

- Responding to change over following a plan

Scrum methodology is a tool that is here to help. Creating beautiful burndowns and using the latest buzz words, acronyms, and techniques is not the goal. The goal is to deliver great software that the customer actually wants and needs—at the highest quality; in the most optimal way; in the most motivating, performant, and dynamic work environment. The key is a self-governing, cross-functional team that improves from iteration to iteration and is fun to be a member of.

Religiously following different methods and techniques is not the goal.

The Scrum Master role is a servant-leader who has no authority. The ScMa concentrates on processes and continuous improvement.

© Ilya Bibik 2018
I. Bibik, *How to Kill the Scrum Monster*, https://doi.org/10.1007/978-1-4842-3691-8_6

The ScMa is like a mechanic who does adjustments and tune-ups of the engine, and at the same time is the oil in the engine that makes everything run smoothly and not wear out over duration of time.

It is critical for the team that the ScMa will not be trapped in administrative tasks and create a Scrum monster, but will help the team to develop into the performing stage and will help the team to kill it's scrum Monster, or even better prevent it from being born in the first place.

Case Studies

The fictional case studies in this appendix present common problems a Scrum team may encounter. I'll guide you through the situation's background, root cause, possible solutions, and the resulting outcome. The solution I've selected isn't necessarily the best one, but it's the one I thought would work best for the fictional Scrum team. Though the situations and characters are fictional, you will find that they will sound familiar and relatable. The goal of this appendix is not to tell you what to do if you find yourself in a similar situation— everyone's situation is unique —but to give you material to reflect on and inspire you to come to your own conclusion.

Situation 1: A Team Member Is Taking Over Responsibilities of Another Role (Not in Order to Help)

Background

Mike is the Scrum Master (ScMa) of a team that consists in part of a team of five junior developers, a senior developer (John), and an Architect (Jack). Mike and the developers work on-site, while the Architect works remotely. The most senior developer, John, feels that because Jack works apart from the rest of the team, it takes Jack longer to accomplish his duties and negatively impacts the team's overall productivity. John thinks he can do a better job than Jack. To compensate for Jack's slowness, John takes it upon himself to make Architect decisions, overriding Jack. John's decisions are often wrong and they mainly contradict what was communicated from Jack. This results in

© Ilya Bibik 2018
I. Bibik, *How to Kill the Scrum Monster*, https://doi.org/10.1007/978-1-4842-3691-8

information coming from two different channels: the senior developer and the Architect. This duplicity causes confusion for the junior developers because they do not know whose guidelines to follow. It also makes the work disorganized, prolongs planning, and negatively affects capacity. The capacity of the ScMa and Product Owner (PO) are affected as well, due to the constant tension between the senior developer and the remote Architect.

Root Cause

Having a remote Architect is not ideal, but the main reason for the problem is the fact that the senior developer, John, is not a team player and has an alternative motive. Instead of having the project's success as top priority, he uses it as an opportunity to promote himself to the role of the Architect and to gain visibility with external stakeholders.

Possible Solutions

A. *Replace the remote Architect with the senior dev.*

B. *Influence the senior dev in order to change his behavior.*

C. *Relocate the remote Architect closer to the team or replace with a new local Architect.*

D. *Remove the senior dev. from the team to avoid conflicts.*

Decision

C. *Relocate the remote Architect closer to the team or replace with a new local Architect.*

Mike was able to persuade Jack to relocate closer to the team so he could work on-site. Now that the entire team is together, there are no more miscommunications. John eventually left to join another team, this time as an Architect.

Situation 2: Ineffective Meeting Planning

Background

The team consists of six senior developers, a senior Architect (Julia), PO Hannah, and a relatively junior ScMa (Michael).

During the planning meetings, the team tends to have discussions about the smallest details of each of the tasks. Oftentimes, due to these discussions, the team achieves minimal to no added value from additional time added to the planning. The planning meetings also become very long and boring. It seems like the big picture gets lost in mostly unnecessary details in these meetings.

Root Cause

The Architect of the team, Julia, is extremely detail oriented and goes much too deep into unnecessary technicalities during planning. All the team members use this as an opportunity to impress Julia and follow suit, rather than providing constructive input. The ScMa is unable to moderate the meeting efficiently. However, Julia tends to be reasonable and practical when she is in a one-on-one planning meeting.

Possible Solutions

A. *Replace the Architect with someone who will be more efficient during planning.*

B. *Replace the ScMa with someone who will be more efficient in moderating the Architect and the team during planning.*

C. *Invite an additional moderator to the meeting to help the ScMa put the meeting back on track when the team reverts to nitpicking.*

D. *ScMa Michael should organize a short preplanning session with the PO and the Architect before the meeting.*

Decision

D. *ScMa Michael should organize a short pre-planning session with the PO and the Architect before the meeting..*

With this solution, the ScMa will save up to 60% to 70% of planning time by making all the crucial decisions beforehand, compelling every member of the team during the planning meeting to focus more on the big picture.

Situation 3: Quality Expert Constantly Misses Deadlines

Background

In the new Scrum team with ScMa Sharon and Quality Manager Bob, QM Bob constantly misses the deadlines for Quality deliverables and only starts working right before the deadline, during the Sprints. To help him catch up, some of the developers have to assist Bob when Quality process escalations occur. This creates additional stress for the team.

Root Cause

QE Bob's working habits create this situation. Additionally, QM Bob is protective of the Quality process and does not allow other roles like the PO and the ScMa to be involved.

Possible Solutions

A. Replace QM Bob.

B. Add an additional QM to the team.

C. Convert one of the developers to the QM role.

D. ScMa Sharon should learn the Quality process and take part of the Quality responsibilities herself, thereby creating pressure on QM Bob to step up.

Decision

D. ScMa Sharon should learn the Quality process and take part of the Quality responsibilities herself, thereby creating pressure on QM Bob to step up.

As a result of this, QM Bob doesn't have a monopoly on Quality responsibilities, which will force Bob to do better. Eventually Sharon will stop being involved in Quality responsibilities after Bob raisees his game.

Situation 4: Another Team Is Trying to Take Over

Background

Team A completed its current project creating a Fashion app. Therefore, management decided to use this team to assist another team, Team B, which has been working on a big and complicated project for the last three years. Team A is completely dependent on Team B with regard to knowledge about the project and technologies used.

The Team B PO (Evan) micromanaged his team and attempts to establish the same processes within Team A. This creates conflict between Team B PO Evan and the ScMa of Team A (Mariana).

While Mariana is trying to stick to Agile principles in the team, Evan is trying to use different processes, his personal connections, and company politics to take over. This creates tension within the team and with ScMa Mariana. The overall productivity of Team A decreases due to inefficient micromanagement, and many members of the team leave.

Root Cause

In this situation, the line management should have intervened. The PO of Team B, Evan, has gained political weight in the company, and line management might be too weak to control the situation. PO Evan tries to gain more weight in the company in order to boost his career by having more teams under his immediate control, even it is not part of his role description.

Possible Solutions

A. Replace PO Evan.

B. Separate the teams and make them work on different projects.

C. Introduce an ombudsman/project manager who will manage the project but not be part of any team.

D. Remove Mariana from the team and have a new ScMa for Team A who will not stick to Agile principles and will allow Evan to micromanage the team.

Decision

If it's not possible to replace PO Evan (Solution A), the only solution is:

C. Introduce an ombudsman/project manager whot will manage the project but not be part of any team.

This way, despite introduction of a new role, the balance between the teams can be achieved, and productivity and team dynamics will be improved

Situation 5: Micromanaging Line Manager

Description

Line Manager Rae has been a PO in the past, and therefore tries to micromanage the team and team processes. This is frustrating for the ScMa and the PO in the team. The team is not functioning well because the developers bypass the ScMa and PO to work directly with Line Manager Rae, as Rae has more authority because he is a direct manager of all the team members. As a result, the team struggles to deliver and constantly works in escalation mode.

Root Cause

Line Manager Rae doesn't understand the Agile and Scrum methodology.

Possible Solutions

A. Replace Line Manager Rae.

B. Escalate the situation to higher management.

C. The ScMa and PO should confront the Line Manager.

Decision

All of the solutions can be done in escalating steps.

B. Escalate the situation to higher management.

C. The ScMa and PO should confront the Line Manager.

A. Replace Line Manager Rae.

Situation 6: One of the Developers Rejects the ScMa

Description

The team has five developers and the ScMa. One of the developers, Anna, rejects the ScMa of the team, Michael. Anna ignores the ScMa during meetings and constantly shows a lack of respect when she interacts with Michael. It creates a problem within team dynamics and a disconnect between Anna and Michael.

Root Cause

Anna doesn't understand the principles and methodologies of Agile Scrum, and the role of the ScMa. She is a very good developer. She is very technical and focuses mainly on the deliverables. She doesn't see outside of her responsibilities. Since Anna knows that ScMa Michael is not writing code, she assumes he is not contributing to the team and is annoyed with his presence.

On the other side, Michael is unable to communicate to Anna what his role is and how critical his contribution is to the team.

Possible Solutions

A. Involve the Line Manager to try to coach Anna and mitigate between Anna and Michael.

B. Ignore the situation and minimize the damage and interruption.

C. Michael should reach out to Anna directly to talk to her about his role in the team. Perhaps Anna could shadow him for a day.

D. Move either Anna or Michael to different team.

Decision

C. Michael should reach out to Anna directly to talk to her about his role in the team. Perhaps Anna could shadow him for a day.

And if it doesn't work, then

A. Involve the Line Manager to try to coach Anna and mitigate between Anna and Michael.

Both Anna and Michael are trying to do their best to contribute to the team goals. The only problem is misperception and miscommunication. It is challenging to change someone's perception, but it is possible.

Situation 7: PO Isolates Himself from the Team (PO Doesn't Want to be Part of the Team)

Description

PO Evan feels "superior" to his team. He physically tries not to sit with his team. He is very formal with them. As a result, it doesn't feel like Evan is part of the team. There is a growing frustration between the team and the PO. The PO blames the team and the team blames PO. The ScMa of the team (Mariana) tries to be the link between the PO and the team, but PO Evan also keeps her at a distance.

Root Cause

PO Evan is not a team player and has communication issues. PO Evan doesn't see team success as his own success but mainly worries about how higher management would perceive him. His first goal is to look good and to be able to justify the failure of the project by blaming it on the team.

Possible Solutions

A. Remove PO Evan from the team.

B. The Line Manager should coach PO Evan.

C. Appoint an external coach to help to solve the situation.

Decision

A. Remove PO Evan from the team.

Usually, if the individual is not a team player, it is very difficult to change this pattern. There is a good chance that discussions and coaching will just extend the agony while other team members leave during the process.

Situation 8: Conflict Between Teams

Team B has been working on a certain project for the last four years when Team A recently joins the project. Team B is under a lot of stress to deliver and the same is expected from Team A. Very minimal knowledge transfer has been organized from Team B to Team A. As a result, Team A is constantly reaching out to Team B with requests for information. Many team members in key roles on Team B complain that this distracts them from work. This problem affects the good relationship between the teams and prevents Team A from delivering in a timely manner.

Root Cause

The cause was not actually that Team B is distracted by Team A, but that certain individuals in the team are trying to cover missed deadlines by using Team A as an excuse.

Possible Solutions

A. Organize additional KT sessions if required.

B. Have certain times blocked off during the week for questions and reduce this time from planning.

C. Identify the root cause and ask the Line Manager to get involved.

D. Use a tool like Jira to allow Team A to ask their questions and for Team B to address those in a timely manner by tracking the response time.

Decision

A. Organize additional KT sessions if required.

B. Have certain times blocked off during the week for questions and reduce this time from planning.

These two solutions involve interaction among team members, and direct interaction is a more effective method of information exchange over tool usage. On the other hand, it will be very difficult to identify and resolve the actual root cause in this case.

Situation 9: Lack of Resources in the Team

Description

Recently, a few key players of Team A left the company. Team A's current project is not a priority for the company, so the company has not filled the empty positions. Team A must still deliver the same amount of work, but with a reduced headcount. As a result, team morale is low and team members have no motivation to work and deliver.

Root Cause

Management failed to shift Team A toward a project that is more suitable for the team's current headcount and motivate the team with new goals and future plans.

Possible Solutions

A. Get a new project to the team and increase headcount.

B. Because Team A is part of a big corporation, they have the ability to increase capacity by getting interns into the team and some other programs that allow them to receive additional headcount using other budgets.

C. Ideate and try to start an exciting project from the team and propose it to higher management.

Decision

All of the possible solutions.

The ideal solution would be to get a new project to the team and increase headcount (Solution A). However, this is not always possible. For this reason, Team A can ideate and try to start a more exciting project from the team and propose it to higher management (Solution C). Then they can try to get some fresh blood into the team (B. Because team A is part of a big corporation, there are ways to increase capacity by getting interns into the team and some other programs that allow them to receive additional headcount using other budgets).

Situation 10: Lack of Senior Developers in the Teams

Description

A new team was just established, primarily with early talents with little experience. The only people with experience in the team are the PO, Architect, and ScMa. As result, it is difficult for the team to self-organize, because the decisions made by all the team members often are not beneficial to the team and company due to lack of experience. This also creates problems on delivering in time and quality.

Root Cause

Senior management decided to save on costs by hiring mainly early talents—fresh out of school, motivated individuals.

Possible Solutions

A. Let junior members make mistakes and learn from the mistakes.

B. Coach more junior team members and emphasize the opinions of the more experienced team members.

Decision

B. Coach more junior team members and emphasize the opinions of the more experienced team members.

Because junior team members do not have the breadth of experience, their decisions may not be the most effective ones or may introduce new issues. In some cases, the best lessons are learned from making mistakes. However, you also need to consider the consequences of those mistakes. If the survival of the company, project, or team is at stake, intentionally allowing mistakes might not be a good idea.

Situation 11: Team Rejects Agile Scrum Methodology

Description

Company ABC wants to switch from the Waterfall methodology to Agile Scrum. External resources were brought in to coach the team on Agile Scrum methodologies. Despite that, the team still rejects the concept of Scrum and is not motivated to comply and be cooperative.

The team hired experienced ScMa Basil, who is familiar with Scrum methodologies. However, because the team is not cooperative, it is very hard for Basil to shift the team's mindset.

Team PO Mariana is also not a big enthusiast of Agile methodology, but she is willing to have a dialog with Basil.

Root Cause

Resistance to change: When an individual or group is used to doing things in a certain way, it is very difficult to shift perceptions and consider that things have to be done differently.

Possible Solutions

A. Hire more developers who have worked with Agile Scrum before and add them to the team.

B. Allow the team to continue working in the way they are familiar with, and slowly and gradually introduce some elements of Agile Scrum in each iteration.

C. Force the team to shift to Agile and ask management for punitive measures against those who will not cooperate.

Decision

B. *Allow the team to continue working in the way they are familiar with, and slowly and gradually introduce some elements of Agile Scrum in each iteration.*

This way you will not introduce too many changes at once, and resistance to change will be less strong.

Situation 12: Team Wants to Have Longer Sprints of Four Weeks

Description

The team is currently operating with four-week Sprints. It was determined that two-week Sprints are much more efficient and productive in the current situation. Despite that, the team wants to have longer Sprints of four or more weeks.

Root Cause

Review meetings and deadlines are an element of stress to the team, so it is natural that team members will try to delay this stress point by increasing the time between the meetings and deadlines. This gives them additional time to go without dealing with this stress. The root causes for it are emotions and fears of not being validated.

Possible Solutions

A. *Have the team operate with four-week Sprint duration.*

B. *Have the ScMa try to convince the team about the benefits of shorter Sprints.*

C. *Have the PO explain to the team that velocity will be reduced without any benefits to the team or product.*

Decision

C and B.

It is often difficult to appeal to reason when emotions are involved. For this reason, in certain situations some framework that is imposed on the team is beneficial. But this is a very sensitive topic because Agile Scrum methodology is team-centric, so other than very obvious situations team self-organization should not be affected.

Situation 13: Developer in the Team Will Work on Other Developers Tasks Instead of His/Her Own

Description

Instead of working on tasks that he committed to completing during planning, Junior developer Alex decided to help with developer Alice's tasks because hers are more exciting and he will learn something new. As a result, the tasks that were assigned to Alex are not being executed, and the team will not be able to deliver what was planned during the planning meeting

Root Cause

Alex is not acting as a team player. He is putting his personal interests above those of the team.

Possible Solutions

A. *The ScMa will get involved during the Sprint and discuss the matter with junior developer Alex*

B. *Wait until the end of the Sprint and bring up the concern during the retrospective.*

C. *Involve the Line Manager in order to influence junior developer Alex to perform his tasks according to his current job responsibilities.*

Decision

A. *The ScMa will get involved during the Sprint and discuss the matter with junior developer Alex.*

It is always better to solve the problem individually instead of creating an uncomfortable situation for your team members. However, if discussing the issue with Alex individually does not help, options B and C will have to follow.

Situation 14: PO Fails to Provide Requirements

Description

PO Evan is not providing final requirements until the project development is over. The team is not happy with this because without getting the final requirements earlier, it makes it challenging to deliver in situations of uncertainty. This also destabilizes the dynamics of the team.

Root Cause

PO Evan is overdefensive and is afraid to release requirements that can contain some uncertainties or errors. By producing the requirements document at the end of the process, PO Evan is confident that his requirements are perfect. In addition, the requirements from PO Evan are too detailed (he shifts into the domain of the design document). As such, it takes a long time to prepare such a detailed requirements document.

Possible Solutions

A. *Make the requirements less detailed.*

B. *Do not start development until the requirement document is provided.*

C. *Discuss with the team the minimum viable scope for requirements.*

Decision

All of the possible solutions will solve the problem if taken in steps.

As the first step, discuss with the team the minimum viable scope for requirements to be provided before development starts (Solutions B and C). Then make this decision transparent to all stakeholders. As the second step, communicate to the PO the required details minimal level (Solution A).

Situation 15: Requirements Change During Sprint

Description

In the middle of the Sprint, PO Evan received new information from the customer that changed all of the project requirements. The team is confused and upset, and they blame PO Evan for the requirements change.

Root Cause

It can happen that requirements change and, if there is no clear process on what to do in such situations, it can demoralize the team and reduce team dynamics and velocity.

Possible Solutions

A. Wait untill the Sprint ends and have a review meeting, and take the new requirements from there.

B. Stop the Sprint and have a new planning meeting, then resume the Sprint with the new plan.

C. Have a review meeting with the PO to see where the team currently is, and based on this review decide on the scope and time for new planning.

Decision

C. Have a review meeting with the PO to see where the team currently is, and based on this review decide on the scope and time for new planning.

Each situation is different and has to be reviewed and aligned on a case by case basis. For example, certain backlogs that are almost completed could make sense to be finalized even if they are not in current requirements. The PO should be transparent with the team, and plan with the ScMa and Line Manager how to keep up the positive spirit in the team.

Situation 16: External Stakeholders Try to Change Requirements Directly With Developers

Description

The team has an inexperienced PO named Lucy. Because Lucy is not experienced or confident in her abilities, Chief PO (CPO) Hannah and Line Manager Wolf do not take Lucy very seriously. They reach out to the team members directly during the Sprint and change the requirements on the fly on a daily basis.

This creates major issues in the team because they are not able to deliver any Sprint completely and backlogs are dragged from Sprint to Sprint. ScMa Michael is not interfering because he is afraid to have bad blood with his Line Manager, who is part of the problem.

Root Cause

The team has no single point of truth, and it makes it impossible to work effectively.

Possible Solutions

A. Discuss the situation with the team and explain the problem and root cause, and have a clear plan of action on how to push back on Hannah and Wolf.

B. Escalate to other stakeholders.

C. Have a meeting with CPO Hannah and Line Manager Wolf, together with the team and all the stakeholders, and come up with a solution.

Decision

All of the possible solutions.

This is a situation where the team has lost control. This problem can be overcome if the team sticks together and supports PO Lucy, even if she is inexperienced (it will build her confidence).

Situation 17: Not Able to Complete Quality DoD During the Sprint

Description

Development usually runs until the end of the Sprint, and often QE Keith is not able to test all the backlogs and give their status during the review meetings.

Root Cause

When developers plan, they may plan until the end of the Sprint without taking into account the needed testing time.

Possible Solutions

A. Developers deliver less during the Sprint, and reserve some time during the Sprint for testing and help the tester to execute the tests.

B. Developers complete the development some time before the end of the Sprint and right away start working on preparations for development of the next Sprint.

C. Execute the testing in N+1 mode; that means the team works on Sprint N+1 while QE Keith executes tests for previous Sprint N.

Decision

C. Execute the testing in N+1 mode; that means the team works on Sprint N+1 while QE Keith executes tests for previous Sprint N.

The cleanest way is Solution C. It is not "by the book" because Scrum is expected to deliver tested software at the end of each Sprint, but it will still work.

Situation 18: A Lot of Nonconstructive Feedback During Retrospective

Description

During retrospective meetings, several team members bring up many opinions about points of improvement that are not relevant to the meeting. As a result, it is challenging and risky to accommodate all the changes during the next Sprint.

Root Cause

Each team member wants to be heard and noticed with what they think are helpful opinions.

Possible Solutions

A. Ask the team to come up with only one point of improvement for the next Sprint.

B. Filter all the points until the team agrees on the most important one to three points.

C. List all the improvement points somewhere and try to execute them during the Sprint.

Decision

A. Ask the team to come up with only one point of improvement for the next Sprint.

B. Filter all the points until the team agrees on the most important one to three points.

Solutions A and B will work. The important thing is to not go for Solution C, because having too many process changes during one Sprint can create potential issues and also is difficult to execute.

Situation 19: Lack of Participation During Retrospective

Description

The team doesn't believe in retrospectives because they see them as boring and a waste of time. They have two-week Sprints, so they have retrospectives twice a month. Usually, all the team members are disengaged during this meeting and ScMa Michael is unable to engage team participation.

Root Cause

The team doesn't see value from the retrospective meetings and they don't feel comfortable venting their thoughts during the meetings.

Possible Solutions

A Have a retrospective meeting every second Sprint to reduce retrospective frequency.

B. ScMa Michael prepares something different for each retrospective meeting.

C. Use the retrospective as a postmortem meeting.

D. Turn around the retrospective and use this meeting occasionally as a team hour for games and entertainment, and ask the team to come up with one action item.

Decision

All of the possible solutions.

There are many techniques on how to execute retrospectives and it is important to give the opportunity to the team to reflect and vent out.

Situation 20: Justified Negative Feedback from Stakeholders During Review

Description

During the review meeting, the team receives negative feedback from stakeholders. The stakeholders notice a mismatch between demo and required functionalities. As a result, the team feels that they didn't do a good job and becomes unmotivated. ScMa Michael and PO Evan act defensive during the meeting, which agitates the stakeholders and makes things even worse.

Root Cause

PO Evan did not specify the exact requirements. Also, the team did not ask the right questions from the PO.

Possible Solutions

A. *ScMa Michael steps in during the meeting and to thank the stakeholders for feedback, and to ensure issues will be investigated and progress will be reported for the next Sprint*

B. *The team makes it part of the process and includes feedback from review in the next planning as action items.*

C. *ScMa Michael notes feedback during the meeting and brings it to the team during an internal meeting.*

Decision

All of the possible solutions.

If taken seriously, most of the negative feedback can be turned around as value added to the team. It is important to show the stakeholders that their feedback is taken seriously, and to show the team that it is business as usual and they are not under attack. The ScMa and PO Evan should protect the team.

Situation 21: Unjustified Negative Feedback from Stakeholders During Review

Description

During a meeting one of the stakeholders, CPO Mary, attacks the team without any particular grounds. Team member John, who developed a particular functionality, falls under Mary's extremely aggressive attack and tries to justify himself. This takes down team spirit and creates negative dynamics.

Root Cause

Mary tries to punish the team because the team reports to the Line Manager she has problems with. She thinks she will punish this manager by attacking his team.

Possible Solutions

A. The ScMa or PO escalates and stops the meeting.

B. The ScMa or PO steps in to accept the feedback and ensure Mary that the issue will be addressed next Sprint, and then produces an email with relevant people on CC that will deal with this issue prior to the next review.

C. The ScMa and PO do not get involved and let the attacked developer handle the situation with CPO Mary.

D. The ScMa and PO escalate the situation after the meeting to their Line Manager.

Decision

Because the ScMa has to protect the team, he has to step in and protect his developer, John. For this reason, the correct solution is B ("*The ScMa or PO steps in to accept the feedback and ensure Mary that the issue will be addressed next Sprint, and then produces an email with relevant people on CC that will deal with this issue prior to the next review*").

At the same time, the ScMa and PO should try to prevent the issue from repeating itself, by escalating it to their line manager. So, their next step will be D ("*The ScMa and PO escalate the situation after the meeting to their Line Manager*").

And as a final resort, if the problem repeats itself at every review meeting and after discussion with the Line Manager, the ScMa and PO can escalate the situation to all the stakeholders, explaining the possible impacts of this situation (Solution D).

Situation 22: Unrealistic Estimates During Planning

Description

The team provides very inaccurate time estimates for tasks. They usually underestimate development tasks and overestimate Quality tasks. As a result, the team is usually not able to deliver during Sprints.

Root Cause

When developers produce estimates for their tasks they don't want to look bad in front of each other, so they produce numbers on the lower side. On the other hand, when QEs work alone, there is no one to challenge the numbers.

Possible Solutions

A. Instead of producing number estimates, ask for the complexity of the task/backlogs used. Often, Story points are used in Agile Scrum to estimate the complexity and then have an average of Story points the team can take during a Sprint.

B. Do not produce any estimates in hours; instead, preassign tasks to developers, and during planning the developers will just commit to certain tasks without assigning any number to them.

C. Add a buffer of N% for each task for each task estimate.

Decision

All of the possible solutions can work.

However, Solution B ("Do not produce any estimates in hours; instead, preassign tasks to developers, and during planning the developers will just commit to certain tasks without assigning any number to them") works best with a self-driven and motivated team, but has the disadvantage of not having measurable values during the Sprint.

Situation 23: Can't Complete Sprint Commitments

Description

In the middle of the Sprint, ScMa Michael realizes the team will not be able to complete all the development tasks it has committed to during the Sprint planning.

Root Cause

The team hasn't accounted for all the efforts during the planning, and misjudged the effort required for the execution.

Possible Solutions

A. ScMa Michael, together with the PO, mitigate possible risks of the missed timelines.

B. ScMa Michael collects information he will be able to present during the review meeting that will explain why the team was not able to complete its commitments.

C. ScMa Michael, together with the PO, try to prioritize the current backlogs assigned to the Sprint in order to achieve maximum value from the Sprint.

D. Request additional capacity.

Decision

The solution will be composed of several steps:

A. ScMa Michael, together with the PO, mitigate possible risks of the missed timelines.

B. ScMa Michael collects information he will be able to present during the review meeting that will explain why the team was not able to complete its commitments.

C. ScMa Michael, together with the PO, try to prioritize the current backlogs assigned to the Sprint in order to achieve maximum value from the Sprint

It makes no sense to add additional resources in the middle of the Sprint (Solution D). It is most likely that the opposite will happen, because adding capacity will reduce existing productivity due to disruption.

Index

A

Agile Manifesto principles, 4

Agile methodologies
  Kanban, 9–11
  Scrum, 11–12
  XP, 8–9

Agile software development, 3

B

Backlog grooming, 21

C

Continuous improvement, 16

D

Definition of Done (DoD), 22–23

Developers, 18, 33, 42–43

E, F, G, H, I, J

eXtreme programming (XP), 7–9

K

Kanban, 7, 9–11

L

Lean, 13

M, N, O

Meetings, 19–21

P

Planning process, 21

Product Owner (PO), 17, 34, 42, 43, 54

Project manager (PM), 32

Q, R

Quality Engineer (QE), 18, 42

Quality Manager (QM), 18, 44

S

Scrum, 7, 11–12

Scrum iterations, 15

Scrum Master (ScMa)
  admin work trap, 32
  agile methodologies, 63 64
  assist another team, 56–57
  change resistance, 36–37
  commitment, tasks, 35
  confidence, 37
  conflicts
    healthy conflict, 47
    instinctual drives (human nature), 46
    miscommunication, 47
    pure evil (political games), 46
    teams, 60–61
    techniques, solving, 48
  deadlines, 55–56
  developers reject, 58
  estimating and monitoring, team, 36
  external stakeholders, 67
  ineffective planning, 54–55

© Ilya Bibik 2018

I. Bibik, *How to Kill the Scrum Monster*, https://doi.org/10.1007/978-1-4842-3691-8

Scrum Master (ScMa) (*cont.*)
　　influence without authority, 32
　　lack of resources, 61–62
　　lack of senior developers, 62
　　Line Manager, 57–58
　　perceptions, personalities, and
　　　　conditions, 34
　　PM, 37–38
　　PO
　　　　fails to provide requirements, 65–66
　　　　isolation, 59–60
　　retrospective
　　　　lack of participation, 70
　　　　nonconstructive feedback, 69
　　roles, combinations
　　　　developer, 33
　　　　line manager, 33
　　　　product owner/business analyst, 34
　　　　quality, 33
　　Sprint
　　　　changing requirements, 66–67
　　　　commitments, 73–74
　　　　DoD, 68–69
　　　　of four weeks, 64
　　stakeholders, negative feedback, 70–71
　　team member, 53–54
　　technical skills, 35
　　unrealistic estimates, 72–73
　　working on other tasks, 65
Scrum methodology
　　agile principals, 28
　　blocks and impediments, 25
　　board, 23–24
　　DoD, 22–23
　　early adoption, 16
　　inspection, 28
　　planning process, 21
　　ScMa, 17
　　self-containing and self-managing team, 16
　　sprint cycle and meetings, 19–20

　　team roles, 17
　　team rules, 24–25
　　tools, 27–28
　　transparency, 16
　　velocity, 25–26
Scrum misuse, 5
Sprint Cycle, 19–20
Sprints, 15

T, U

Team dynamics
　　conflict/problems resolutions, 45
　　external-to-team communications
　　　　line manager, 44
　　　　team–program, 44
　　　　team–stakeholders, 44–45
　　forming, 39
　　norming, 40
　　performing, 40
　　relationships between roles
　　　　architect–developers, 42
　　　　Architect–PO/Architect–ScMa, 42
　　　　PO–team, 43
　　　　ScMa and PO, 42
　　　　ScMa-QE, 42
　　　　scrum master–developers, 43
　　　　technical writer–team, 43
　　storming, 39
Technical writer, 18
Transparency, 16

V

Values, Agile Manifesto, 51

W, X, Y, Z

Waterfall model, 2
Waterfall *vs.* Agile, 2

Printed in the United States
By Bookmasters